Shark Attack!

By Bob Woods

The
Child's
World®
www.childsworld.com

Published in the United States of America by The Child's World®
P.O. Box 326 • Chanhassen, MN 55317-0326
800-599-READ • www.childsworld.com

ACKNOWLEDGMENTS

The Child's World®: Mary Berendes, Publishing Director

Produced by Shoreline Publishing Group LLC
President / Editorial Director: James Buckley, Jr.
Designer: Tom Carling, carlingdesign.com
Cover Art: Slimfilms
Copy Editor: Beth Adelman

Photo Credits
Cover—Main: Corbis; Insets: Corbis (left), Photos.com (2)
Interior—AP/Wide World: 15, 17, 21, 24, 26; Corbis: 8, 11, 18;
iStock: 1, 4, 6, 7 (bottom), 12, 16, 23; Minden Pictures:
10, 13, 19; Photos.com: 7 (top), 28;

LIBRARY OF CONGRESS CATALOGING-IN-PUBLICATION DATA

Woods, Bob.
  Shark attack! / by Bob Woods.
      p. cm. — (Boys rock!)
  Includes bibliographical references and index.
  ISBN 1-59296-734-5 (library bound : alk. paper)
  1. Shark attacks—Juvenile literature. I. Title. II. Series.
  QL638.93.W66 2006
  597.3—dc22
                              2006001637

CONTENTS

4   CHAPTER 1
Should You Be Afraid?

14   CHAPTER 2
Why Sharks Attack

22   CHAPTER 3
You and Sharks

30   GLOSSARY

31   FIND OUT MORE

32   INDEX

SHOULD YOU BE Afraid?

A quiet day at the beach . . . when suddenly—*SHARK!* Lifeguards' whistles shriek. Panicked swimmers run out of the water. Then everyone stands on the beach, scanning the ocean surface for the telltale fin of the shark!

Nature shows and movies about these man-eating monsters are wildly popular. When there is a shark attack,

the **media** report on it for
days. Some people decide
never to swim at the beach.

As with so many things we
fear, though, the truth about
sharks is not nearly so scary.
Sharks are really not that
dangerous—at least if you're
a human.

Are sharks all bad? Or do they have some good points? Read on to find out.

Sharks began roaming Earth's oceans over 400 million years ago—long before the age of the dinosaurs. Today, *T. rex* is long gone, but sharks such as the great white, tiger shark, and bull shark live on.

Among the 450 types of sharks, those three are involved in most of the attacks on humans.

This fossil shark tooth is more than 100 million years old. Sharks have been around for a long time!

Shark attacks are extremely rare. At the beach, you're at much greater risk of getting hurt from sunburn! You might get stung by a **jellyfish**, cut your foot on a seashell, or get in trouble while you're swimming.

A person's chances of being killed by a shark are very, very small. In the United States, bee and wasp stings cause about 50 deaths each year. Nearly 800 people die from bicycle accidents.

In 2004, exactly *one person* died from a shark attack in the U.S.

Do you want something to worry about? You have a better chance of getting stung by a bee or a jellyfish!

The great white shark, star of the movie *Jaws*, is the most famous type of shark. Its open mouth reveals huge, sharp teeth. A fin shaped like a triangle sits atop its grey, torpedo-shaped body.

Yikes! The mouth of the great white shark is a fearsome sight.

A great white can grow to around 20 feet (6 m) long, weigh 5,000 pounds (2,268 kg), and have 3,000 teeth!

All sharks are fish. The smallest **species** is the dwarf lanternshark, at about six inches (15 cm). The largest is the whale shark, which averages 45 feet (14 m) long and weighs 24,000 pounds (10,886 kg). Also, unlike most fish, sharks don't have bones. Their skeletons are made of **cartilage**—the same tough, flexible tissue that forms your nose and ears.

Scientists have identified more than 450 species, or types, of sharks around the world.

Here's looking at you—from both sides! The hammerhead has a wide, hammer-shaped head.

Most sharks have a narrow body shape with a large tail and a pointed nose. Some sharks have special features. The sawshark has a long, flat snout edged with sharp teeth. And check out the hammerhead's unusual wide head, with an eye on each side!

Tails vary, too. A boomerang shape helps the fastest shark, the mako, reach speeds of up to 60 miles (97 km) per hour. The thresher shark's sword-shaped tail can grow to eight feet (2 m) long.

Many sharks have gray skin. Some have spots or stripes.

The mako shark is one of the fastest fish in the sea.

Most sharks' jaws are filled with rows of sharp, pointed teeth and can open wide— as these jaw bones show.

Sharks have black, green, or gold eyes. They see in color, and have very good eyesight. Their "ears" are actually two tiny openings on top of their heads. Sharks have keen senses of smell and taste, too.

Sharks are **predators**. That

Sharks in the River?

Dangerous bull sharks live not only in warm ocean waters, but also in freshwater rivers. They have been spotted in the Mississippi River, as far north as Illinois!

means they eat other animals. Different kinds of sharks have different kinds of teeth, depending on what foods or prey they eat. For instance, tiger and great white sharks use their super-sharp teeth to rip apart fish, seals, and sea turtles— and, on very rare occasions, people.

The enormous whale shark swims with its mouth open. Its thousands of tiny teeth help it gather up tiny fish and **plankton**.

WHY SHARKS Attack

2

Sharks can be **aggressive** hunters, but they do not hunt for humans. Of the hundreds of shark species, only about 30 are known to have attacked people. Every day, millions of people swim, dive, or fish in waters where sharks live. Even so, only about 50 are attacked each year.

Scientists at the University of Florida have conducted a worldwide study of shark attacks. In 2004, they counted 61 **unprovoked** attacks—those in which the shark, not the person, made first contact. Seven of the 61 victims died.

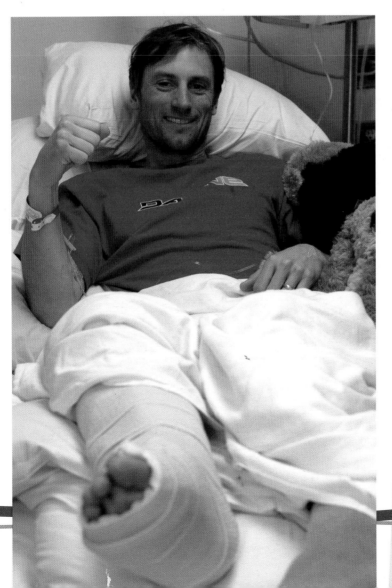

In late 2005, a shark bit surfer Brian Anderson on the foot while Anderson was surfing off the Oregon coast. Brian escaped by bopping the shark on the nose with his fist.

The sight of a shark cruising along can be a scary thing if you're swimming or surfing.

There are two different kinds of unprovoked shark attacks on humans. Most are hit-and-run attacks near beaches. The sharks find fish in these waters, but there are also swimmers, divers, and surfers. Big waves and strong **currents** churn up the shallow water. In those **murky** waters, a shark can mistake a moving human for a fish. Usually, the shark takes a quick bite and moves on. The person's injuries are often minor.

A few bump-and-bite attacks happen in deeper water, where the person doesn't see the shark before it strikes. It might bump the person first, then bite, again and again. Attacks like these can cause serious injury or death.

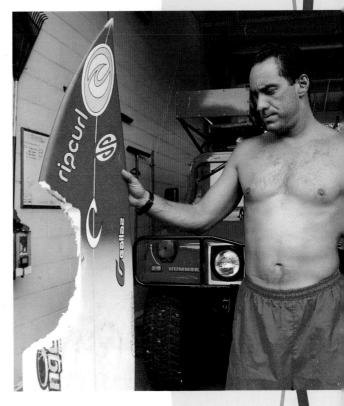

Shark snack: A surfer shows off a surfboard bitten by a great white shark in Hawai'i.

Man in a Cage

Scuba divers can get very close to sharks by protecting themselves with strong metal cages. These cages are used by scientists and photographers.

Although great whites are the most feared sharks, most people who encounter them live to tell their tales. It seems that these sharks don't particularly care for the taste of humans.

Nonetheless, great whites are feared as killers that rip swimmers to shreds.

That's a **myth**. A shark's many teeth and powerful jaws can turn a big, fat seal into fast food, but humans aren't on the great white's menu. If a great white does take a bite out of a person, it usually spits out the piece and moves on. We're too bony!

You may have heard of myths as stories from long ago. In this case, a "myth" is something that is untrue, although many people might believe it.

Sharks most often eat large fish or ocean mammals such as seals.

Tales of surviving shark attacks are both fascinating and frightening. On October 31, 2003, a 14-foot (4-m) tiger shark attacked 13-year-old champion surfer Bethany Hamilton in Hawai'i. She lost her left arm, but not her spirit.

"My arm was hanging in the water and it just came and bit me," she told a reporter. "But I just held onto my board and then it let go." The shark swam away. Luckily, Bethany was surfing with her dad.

Bethany's bravery has made her a hero to many people. She has appeared on many TV shows talking about how she battled back from her injury.

Bethany's bravery in coming back from a shark attack has been an inspiration to many kids.

He quickly got her back to shore and saved her life.

Just 10 weeks later, Bethany was back on a surfboard and getting ready to compete again—and she won!

3

YOU AND
Sharks

The odds of coming face-to-face with a shark are tiny—even if you often go to the beach. But what if you do see one? Would you know how to avoid danger?

Here are some tips from shark experts for whenever you go in the ocean:

- At the beach, don't wander too far from shore.
- Avoid swimming alone. Be sure parents

and lifeguards can see you.

- If the waves are big and the water is murky, don't splash around too much. A shark feeding in the area might mistake you for a fish.

- Avoid going in the water at dawn, at dusk, or after dark, when sharks like to feed.

Ready to hit the waves? Make sure to stay safe when you're at the beach.

- Remove shiny jewelry.
- Don't go in the water if you're bleeding.
- Don't swim, dive, or surf near fishing boats. They often throw bait in the

Everybody out of the water! People on this Florida beach got a close-up look at a visiting shark.

water to attract fish—and sometimes sharks.

- Beware of sitting on a surfboard in deep water. Dangling arms and legs make you look like a seal from underneath.
- Stay out of areas where sharks have been reported in the past few days or where they regularly feed.

Where are sharks? All over the world. Great white sharks appear near beaches in South Africa, Australia, and the Northwest Coast of the United States.

If you do see a shark, never try to touch it. Leave the water immediately. If you are attacked, stay calm. Fight back by punching the shark in the eyes or **gills**.

Sadly, thousands of sharks are killed just for their fins.

As much as we fear sharks, sharks really should fear us more. After all, sharks only kill a few people each year, while people kill millions of sharks. Many shark species are in danger of becoming **extinct**—dying out altogether.

The greatest human threat

to sharks is fishing. Some fisherman catch sharks for sport. Others are after the sharks' cartilage, which is used in some medicines.

In some Asian countries, the fins are cut off live sharks—which are then thrown back into the sea to die—and used to make a special soup.

Endangered Sharks

Scientists have identified nearly twenty species of sharks at risk of becoming extinct because they're hunted for food and body parts. Among them are the basking, whitefin, blacktip, and great white sharks.

Marine biologists and environmental groups are working to protect sharks from human abuse. They also are asking governments around the world to ban unnecessary shark fishing.

"Marine" means having to do with the ocean. Marine biologists study all kinds of life in the ocean, from huge fish to tiny plankton.

Larger sharks—such as great white, basking, and whale sharks—face the greatest danger, because they are the ones humans hunt the most. Great white sharks are now protected along the coasts of California and South Africa. They cannot be hunted in those areas.

We're learning that sharks aren't really the bloodthirsty killers of popular movies. They're really an important and valuable part of their ocean environment.

By learning more about sharks, we can come to respect these ancient animals and their place in the world.

Most sharks do not chew their food. Instead, they gulp it down in large pieces.

GLOSSARY

aggressive someone or something that is mean and is often ready to attack

cartilage flexible, bony material that makes up a shark's body (and your nose and ears)

currents constantly flowing water or air

extinct no longer existing; usually used to describe animals or plants

gills the slits on both sides of a fish's head that it uses to breathe

jellyfish a sea creature that has no backbone and an almost clear body; some have long, stinging tentacles

marine biologists scientists who study animals and plants that live in the sea

media all the television and radio networks, newspapers, magazines, and Web sites that report news, and the people who work for them

murky cloudy or hard to see in

myth a story, often an ancient one; a fictional tale

plankton tiny sea plants and animals that float near the surface and are often eaten by fish

predators animals that hunt other animals

species a group of closely related plants or animals

unprovoked not caused by the person being attacked

FIND OUT MORE

BOOKS

Discovering Sharks and Rays
by Nancy Field
(Dog-Eared Publications, Middleton, WI) 2003
Activities and information about the world of sharks and
their cousins, the rays.

Dolphins and Sharks: A Magic Treehouse Research Guide
by Mary Pope Osborne
(Random House Books for Young Readers, New York) 2004
A nonfiction companion to the well-known fiction series,
this book gives the facts behind the stories.

Shark
by Miranda MacQuitty
(DK Publishing, New York) 2000
Dozens and dozens of photos of sharks of all sorts, including
close-up looks at their bodies and descriptions of their
activities.

WEB SITES

Visit our home page for lots of links about sharks:
www.childsworld.com/links

Note to Parents, Teachers, and Librarians: We routinely check our Web links to
make sure they're safe, active sites—so encourage your readers to check them out!

INDEX

ancient history and fossils, 6

Anderson, Brian, 15

attacks, 14–21, 25

body shape, 10, 11

cages to study sharks from, 18

cartilage, 9, 27

dangers on the beach, 4–5, 6–7

death by shark attack, 7, 15

endangered species, 26–27, 28

eyes and eyesight, 12, 16–17, 25

fastest shark, 11

fear of sharks, 4–5, 18

fin, 8, 26, 27

food and prey, 12–13, 19, 29

freshwater shark, 13

great white shark, 8, 13, 18, 25, 27, 28

Hamilton, Bethany, 20–21

hunting and food gathering, 13, 16–17

largest shark, 9

number of types, 6

safety tips, 22–25

scientists who study sharks, 18, 28

sharks in television and movies, 4–5, 8, 29

size, 9

skin, 11

smallest shark, 9

survivors of shark attack, 15, 20–21

tail, 11

teeth and jaws, 8, 9, 12, 13

types of sharks, 6, 9–11, 13, 27, 28

what to do during attack, 15, 25

BOB WOODS, who is not afraid to go swimming in the ocean, has written many books for young readers and for adults. He has written about many sports, cars and motorcycles, business, and other topics. He lives in Connecticut.